Science Success 1

Terry Jennings

Acknowledgements

The author and publisher would like to thank the following for help in the preparation of this book:

St Peter's CE Infants School, Alvescot, Bampton; Francis Baily Primary School, Thatcham; Manor County Primary School, Uckfield; Linda Trimby; Jeremy Cottam; Sue Ashforth-Smith; Ann Mepham; British Glass Recycling Company; Health Education Authority

Photographic credits

Bo'sun/R D Battersby pp 4 (bottom), 5 (top), 10–11, 12 (top, bottom), 14, 18 (top, bottom), 20 (bottom), 22 (left, right), 24, 25, 28 (left, right), 29 (right), 30 (bottom), 33 (top), 37 (top), 42 (bottom) /L R Miles p 29 (left); picture courtesy of British Glass Recycling Company p 13; James Davis Worldwide p 32; Eye Ubiquitous /Mike Powles p 8 /Steve Lindridge p 27 (left) /Tim Durham p 27 (right) /Bennett Dean p 30 (top) /Yiorgos Nikiteas p 35 /M Accwood-Copin pp 36–37 (bottom) /Howard Brundrett p 43 /E L Neil p 44 (left); picture courtesy of Health Education Authority p 4 (top); Terry Jennings pp 31, 33 (bottom), 39 (left, right), 40; Anthony Blake Photo Library/Maximilian Stock Ltd p 38; Science Photo Library pp 7 (right), 15 /Alex Bartel p 21 /Simon Fraser p 36 (top) /Rosenfeld Images Ltd p 42 (top); Telegraph Colour Library/Neil McIntyre p 9 /Benelux p 44; Tony Stone/Dale Durfee p 7 (left), p 45.

OXFORD
UNIVERSITY PRESS

Great Clarendon Street, Oxford OX2 6DP

Oxford University Press is a department of the University of Oxford. It furthers the University's objective of excellence in research, scholarship, and education by publishing worldwide in

Oxford New York

Auckland Bangkok Buenos Aires Cape Town Chennai Dar es Salaam Delhi Hong Kong Istanbul Karachi Kolkata Kuala Lumpur Madrid Melbourne Mexico City Mumbai Nairobi São Paulo Shanghai Taipei Tokyo Toronto

First published 2000

10 9 8 7 6

ISBN 0 19 918338 4

Editorial, design and picture research by
Lodestone Publishing Limited, Uckfield, East Sussex

Illustrations by David Barnett, Jane Fern, Nick Hawken, John James, Jonathan Satchell, and Dawn Brend

Science consultant: Dr Julian Rowe

Language consultant: Ann Parham

Cover design: Oxford Designers and Illustrators

Printed in Spain by Gráficas Estella

Contents

(and suggested order of teaching)

A balanced diet

The food we eat is called our **diet**. We need different kinds of foods in our diet in order to stay healthy.

A balanced diet means eating foods from different groups. In this way our body gets what it needs to stay healthy. There are three main groups of foods: foods for growth, foods for **activity** and foods that keep us healthy. Our body uses each kind of food in a different way.

These are some of the foods we need for a balanced diet.

Foods for growth

Meat, fish, eggs, cheese, lentils and beans are some foods which help your body to grow and repair itself.

Foods for activity

To be active we need to eat some **starches**, sugar and **fats**. Bread, potatoes, cereals and pasta are starches. Starches and sugar give us **energy**.

Butter, margarine and cooking oil are fats. Fried foods, meat, milk and peanuts contain fats. Fats store energy for your body to use, but you should not eat too much of them.

These foods contain a lot of fibre.

Foods that keep us healthy

Fruit and vegetables contain **vitamins**, **mineral salts** and **fibre**, which we also need for a balanced diet. Vitamins and mineral salts help to keep us healthy so that our body can fight off diseases. Fibre helps to carry the waste food out of our body.

If you feel hungry between meals, try eating some of these foods.

Questions

1 a Make a list of all the foods and drinks you have had today. Write **g** next to the foods for growth. Write **a** next to the foods for activity. Now write **f** next to foods which contain a large amount of fat.

b Which countries do each of the foods come from?

2 Look at the foods and drinks in the box.

fruit	cakes	rice	sweets
vegetables	water	fried foods	
salads	nuts	biscuits	
fizzy drinks	bread	milk	

a Which should you eat for a balanced diet?

b You should eat only a small amount of some of the foods and drinks. Which are they?

3 Design a poster encouraging children to eat sensibly. How could you improve your diet?

4 Find out why some foods are frozen. How was food kept fresh before fridges and freezers were available? Discuss what you have found out with your friends.

Teeth and the food we eat

We use our teeth to bite off the food we eat and to break it up into pieces small enough to swallow. Our teeth also help us to speak clearly.

Brush your teeth after meals and before you go to bed to remove sugary foods and germs that make your teeth *decay*. Visit your dentist regularly for a check-up.

Milk teeth

Most babies younger than six months old do not have teeth. They do not need them because they cannot eat solid food. The first set of teeth has grown by the time a child is two years old. These are called milk teeth and there are 20 of them.

Adult teeth

When a child is about six years old the adult teeth begin to grow. They slowly push out the milk teeth. One by one the second set of teeth, the 32 adult teeth, replace them.

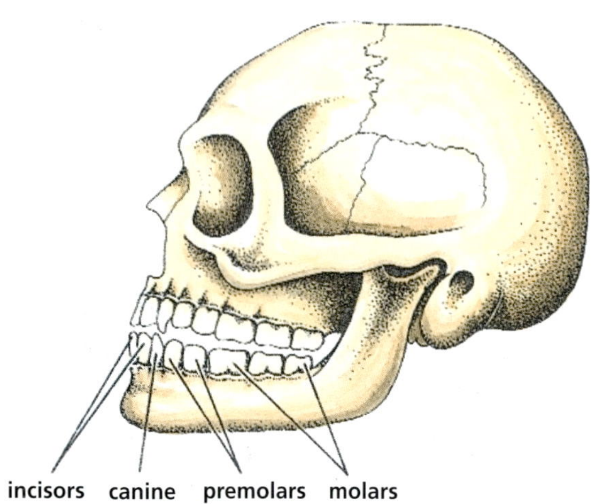

Incisors are sharp and are used for biting food.

Canines are pointed for gripping and tearing food.

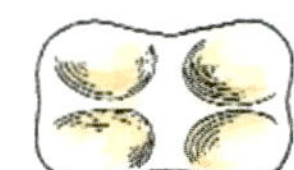
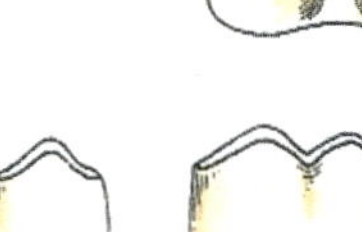
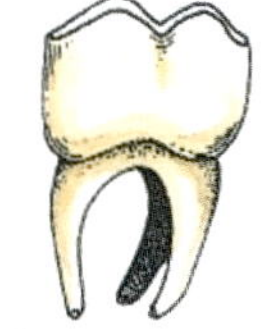

Premolars and molars have flat tops for crushing and grinding food when we chew.

We have four different kinds of teeth, each with a special job to do.

Healthy teeth and gums

Teeth are strong because they have to keep working for many years. Healthy **gums** are as important as healthy teeth. Our gums help to hold our teeth in place. We can keep our teeth and gums healthy by not eating too many sweet or sticky foods, and by brushing them regularly.

We can keep our teeth healthy if we look after them.

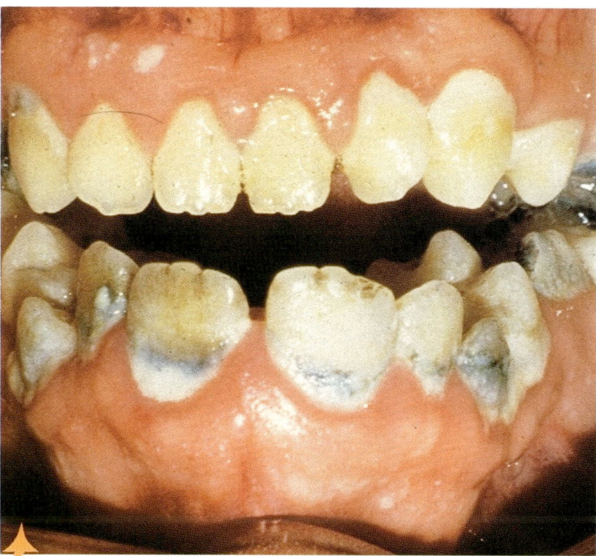

This is what happens if we do not look after our teeth.

Questions

1 Think about each of these things. Do they keep your teeth healthy or harm them? For each answer explain why.
   - a toothbrush
   - b glass of water
   - c toothpaste
   - d sweets
   - e raw carrot or apple

2 Design a poster encouraging children to clean their teeth properly. Do you clean your teeth properly?

3 a Look in a mirror and draw and label your teeth. How many teeth do you have? Which are milk teeth and which are adult teeth?

   b Compare your drawing with your friends' drawings. How are their teeth different from yours?

Animals and their diets

What do tigers eat?

Like us, many animals have teeth which they use for holding, cutting and chewing food. Like ours, their teeth have to be strong. You can tell what an animal eats by looking at its teeth.

Meat-eaters

Animals that eat meat have long, hooked, curved, **canine** teeth which are used to stab **prey**. The **incisors** chop up food and scrape the flesh off bones. The **molars** have sharp edges for cutting up meat and flat surfaces for crushing bones.

Plant-eating animals

Animals, such as sheep, cattle, deer and giraffes, feed on grasses, tree leaves and other plants. These animals grind their food.

Growing teeth

Human teeth stop growing when we are adults, but some animals have teeth that grow all the time. The premolars and molars of plant-eating animals grow all the time so that they don't wear away completely. The incisors of rabbits, mice, gerbils and rats grow all the time. If these animals don't chew hard foods, their front teeth grow so long that they cannot close their mouths.

Squirrels eat hard nuts to wear down their incisors which grow all the time.

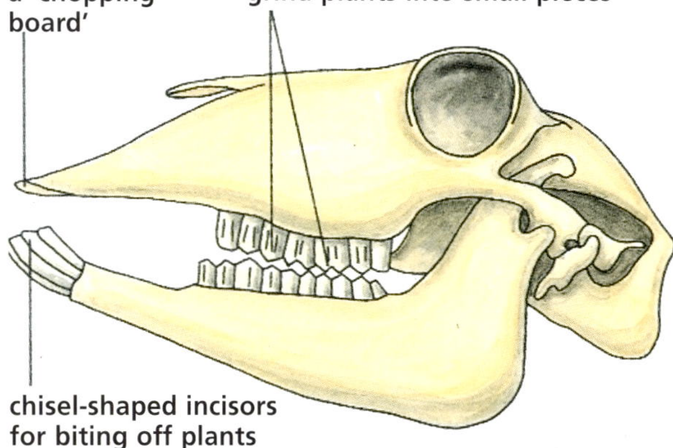

sheep's skull

Why don't plant-eaters have canine teeth?

Questions

1 a Collect pictures of animals. Sort your pictures into 'Animals that eat plants' and 'Animals that eat meat'.
  b Study your pictures. How many ways can you see in which the two groups of animals are different from each other?

2 Copy the list of animals in the box. Write **m** next to the animals that eat meat, and **p** next to the animals that eat plants. Think of more animals to add to your list. Which animals eat plants *and* meat?

rabbit	lion	deer	elephant	fox
cow	tiger	sheep	seal	zebra

3 a Find out what foods a small pet animal such as a mouse, hamster or gerbil eats. Make a list of the foods.
  b What sort of teeth does the animal need for it to be able to eat the foods?

The right material for the job

All over the world people use **materials**. People need food and drink, clothes to wear and homes to live in. They travel from place to place in cars, buses, trains, aircraft or on bicycles. All of these things are made of materials.

Natural materials

There are many thousands of different materials. **Natural materials**, like clay, wood, wool, cotton and rocks, come from plants, animals or from the ground. **Manufactured materials** are made by people from natural substances called **raw materials**. Metals are made from raw materials found in certain rocks. Most **plastics** are made from oil. In this case, oil is a raw material.

Choosing materials

It is important that we use the right material for each job. A window pane made of metal would not be much use because we would not be able to see through it. When we make something, we have to choose materials which have the right **properties**.

What properties do each of these materials have?

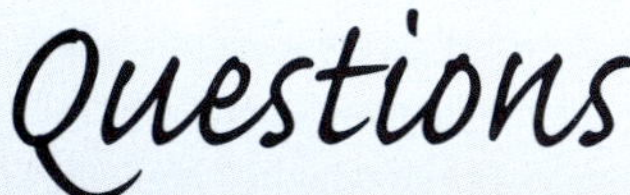

Questions

1 Look at each object in the picture.
   a What is it made from?
   b What properties does the material have?
   c Could the object have been made from a different material? Explain why.

2 Draw a picture of a bicycle. Label the parts. Find out what material each part is made from. Why was each material used?

3 a What materials are used to build houses where you live?
   b Are different building materials used in different parts of the world? Why is this? Collect pictures of houses from different parts of the world. What building materials were used to make the houses? Discuss your pictures with your friends.

What is glass?

Glass is a manufactured material which is made by heating together sand and substances called soda and lime in a **furnace**. The furnace is very hot and the sand, soda and lime melt and mix together to form glass.

What materials could be used instead of glass in these objects? Would these materials be better or worse than glass?

Making bottles

To make bottles and drinking glasses the melted glass is usually poured into moulds and allowed to cool. Some drinking glasses are made by blowing air through a long metal tube into a blob of **molten** glass.

Glass windows and doors

Glass is used in windows because it is **transparent**. This means it lets light through and we can see through it. Glass for windows is made in very large sheets which are then cut to size. The glass used in some doors and car windscreens is toughened so that it will not shatter and splinter if it is broken.

A greenhouse is made from clear glass so that it lets in the sunlight.

More uses of glass

Glass is also used to make mirrors, ornaments, jars and bottles, cooking bowls and dishes. Pure glass is ground into the right shape and polished to make **lenses**. Binoculars, telescopes, cameras, spectacles and microscopes have lenses in them.

Glass fibre

Molten glass can be pulled out into thin threads. When these threads cool they become solid and are bunched together to make glass **fibre**. Glass fibre is used to make some boat hulls, car bodies, fishing rods, curtains and insulation to put in roofs and walls to keep houses warm.

New glass can be made from old glass. This is called recycling.

Questions

1 Cars are made from many different materials.
   - a Why is glass used to make car windows?
   - b Why is rubber used for car tyres?
   - c Why is steel used to make the body of a car?
   - d What other materials are cars made from?

2 What is double glazing? Find out why it is used in modern buildings.

3 In which ways are glass bottles better than plastic bottles? In which ways are plastic bottles better than glass bottles? Discuss this with your friends, then write down your ideas.

Paper

We use paper every day for writing and printing, for wrapping and packing, for tissues, tickets, posters and banknotes. It is even used for some kinds of clothing.

These objects are made from different kinds of paper. What are the properties of each kind of paper?

Wood pulp

Most paper is manufactured from wood. Logs are chopped into small pieces which are boiled with a chemical called caustic soda. This turns the wood chips into a soft pulp.

Wood pulp is drained on a fine sieve to remove some of the water, then it goes into the papermaking machine.

Paper fibres

Paper is made up of lots of tiny **fibres** in the wood pulp. These are pressed together and dried. For many kinds of paper, including banknotes, materials such as cotton rags are added to the wood pulp. These help to make the paper stronger. Chemicals and glues may also be added to bind the fibres together to make the paper even stronger or waterproof. Cardboard is made of thick paper hardened with glue. Writing and drawing paper is made white by bleaching the wood pulp.

The papermaking machine

In the papermaking machine, the pulp is spread over a large moving belt made of finely woven cloth. A lot more of the water is gradually removed from the wood pulp. Then the pulp is pressed between large rollers which squeeze it out into thin sheets. The paper is finished by passing it through heated rollers to make it smooth.

Questions

1 Plan an investigation to test the strength of strips of different kinds of paper which are all the same size.
   a What do you expect to find?
   b Try out your test. Does it work?
   c Was it a fair test?

2 How many different kinds of paper, card and cardboard can you collect? Make a display of them in your classroom. What is each one used for? Why is it used?

3 a Find out which trees give us most of the wood pulp from which paper is made.
   b Why are these trees used?
   c Where are they grown?
   Write a short account of what you have learned.

4 a Why is it a good thing if we recycle used paper?
   b Which things are made of recycled paper?

Everyday plastics

Plastics are made from chemicals that come from oil. Nowadays we use more and more plastics.

There are five common kinds of plastic. Here are a few of the things which can be made from each kind.

Properties of plastics

We often make things from plastics instead of materials like wood, metal and glass. This is because plastics are cheap, easier to use, light, do not rust or rot, and many plastics are difficult to break. Heat does not pass easily through plastics, so they are used for the handles of saucepans and kettles. Electricity does not pass through plastics, so they can be used to cover electrical wires, switches and plugs.

Plastics can be any colour and can be moulded into any shape. Buckets, bowls, bottles, toys, pens, combs and many other everyday things can be made from plastics.

Different kinds of plastics

There are many different kinds of plastics which have thousands of uses. Some are bendy, some are rigid; some are tough, some break easily. Some plastics are transparent like glass; others are **opaque**, which means they do not let light pass through them. Some plastics can be drawn out into fine fibres. Others can be made into flat sheets.

Questions

1. Look around your home or classroom. Make a list of all the things you can see which are made from plastic.
   - **a** Why was plastic used?
   - **b** Could any other material have been used instead?
2. Make a collection of clothes, or pictures of clothes, made from plastics.
   - **a** Why are plastics used for some kinds of clothing?
   - **b** For which kinds of clothing are plastics not suitable?
3. **a** Plan an investigation to test the strength of plastic drinking straws. How will you make sure that your test is fair?
   - **b** Try out your ideas. Does your experiment work?

Magnets push and pull

Magnets come in many shapes and sizes. They are made in factories from iron or steel. Small nails and pins stick to magnets as if they were glued.

Which of these magnets do you think is the strongest? How could you test your ideas?

The magnet attracts the paper clip because the paper clip is made of steel. Which other objects will the magnet attract?

Magnetic materials

Magnets will pull some things towards them. We say these things have been **attracted** to the magnet. Things attracted to magnets are all made of the metals iron, steel, cobalt or nickel. These are called **magnetic** materials. Materials which are not attracted to magnets are said to be non-magnetic.

Attract and repel

The pull, or magnetic **force**, of a magnet is strongest at its ends, or **poles**. One end is a north pole, the other end is a south pole. One magnet sometimes attracts another magnet. The two magnets pull towards each other. If the north pole of one magnet is placed near the south pole of another, the magnets will attract each other.

'Unlike' poles (a north and a south pole) of magnets pull together, or attract, each other.

'Like' poles (two north or two south poles) of magnets push away, or repel, each other.

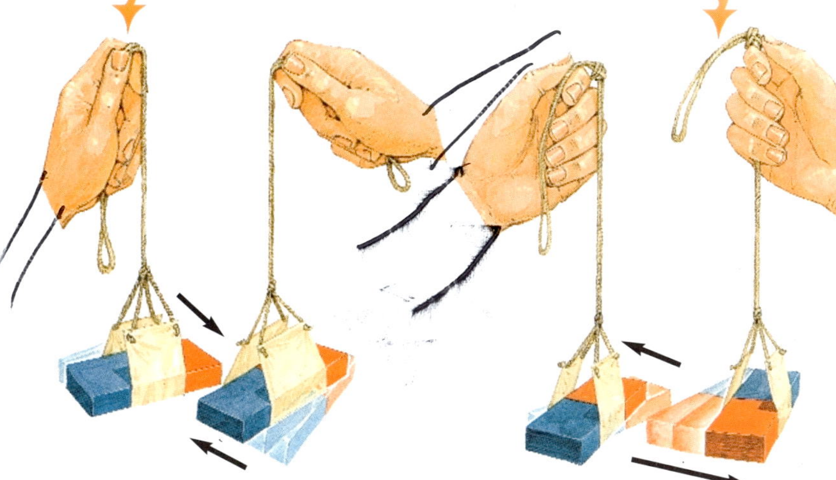

If you put the south pole of one magnet near the south pole of another, they will push each other away. We say the two magnets **repel** each other. In the same way, the north pole of one magnet will repel the north pole of another.

Questions

1 Copy the objects in the box. Put a tick (✔) next to the objects that a magnet will pick up. Put a cross (✘) next to the objects that a magnet will not pick up.

paper clip	safety pin	needle	eraser
small nails	chalk	elastic band	
pencil	bus ticket	cork	

2 Some magnets are stronger than others. Is this because of their size, shape, colour, length or weight, for example? Plan an investigation to find the answer to this question. Is your test fair?

3 The magnetic force of a magnet passes through a piece of paper. You can see this because a magnet will pick up a pin when the pin is under a thin piece of paper. Which other materials will the magnetic force pass through? Plan an investigation to find out.

Using magnets

Magnets can be fun to play with – there are magnets in electric train sets and lots of other toys. We also use magnets in many important ways every day.

Uses of magnets

Magnets are used in radios, television sets, video players, computers, telephones and microphones. There are magnets in electric motors, so vacuum cleaners, refrigerators, freezers and washing machines also have magnets. All the electrically operated, motor-driven parts in a car have a magnet. Magnetic strips built into a refrigerator door keep the door shut.

Power stations

The machines which make electricity in a **power station** are called generators. They have huge magnets in them.

Compasses

There is a magnet in a compass. Compasses are used on ships and aircraft and by explorers for finding the way.

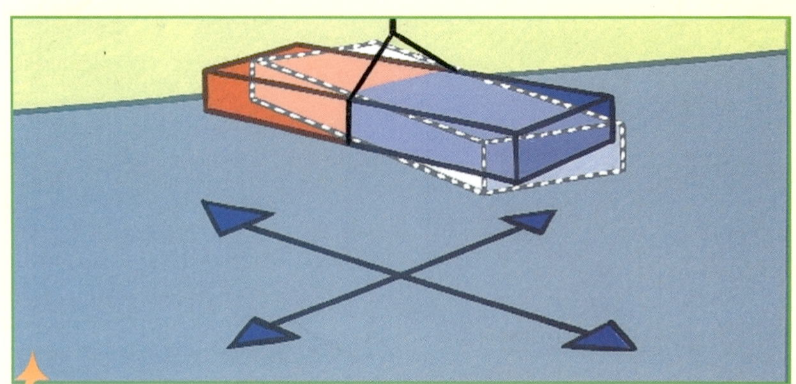

A bar magnet hung from a piece of string will swing around until it points north–south.

A compass needle is a small, thin magnet. The compass needle always points north.

This electromagnet is used to separate and lift heavy iron and steel objects at a scrapyard.

Electromagnets

Cranes with a magnet on them are used to separate iron, steel, cobalt and nickel from other metals at the scrapyard. These magnets are worked by electricity so they are called **electromagnets**. Steel cans for **recycling** can be separated from aluminium cans using an electromagnet.

Questions

1 a Design a fishing game that uses magnets.
  b Describe what materials you will use for the rod and line.
  c What material will you use for the fish?
  d How can you make the magnet 'catch' the fish?
  e How will you decide who is the winner of your fishing game?

2 Copy these sentences. Put a tick (✔) next to the sentences that are true. Put a cross (✘) next to the sentences that are false.
  a Magnets attract only shiny things.
  b Repel means to push away.
  c A compass always points east.
  d Magnets are dangerous to touch.
  e If you drop a magnet, it can stop working.

3 How could you use a magnet to move a metal toy car across the table without touching it? Draw a labelled picture to show what you would do.

Springs and things

When two magnets pull or push each other we say that they exert a **force**. As well as pulling or pushing things, forces can squash or stretch things. We can stretch an elastic band by pulling on each end, and we can squeeze a sponge by pushing its sides.

Pulling and stretching

The more we pull on the ends of an elastic band, the bigger the force that is pulling on it and the more it stretches. If the force is too big, the elastic band will break. Some materials break easily if we try to stretch them. Others need a huge force to break them.

Springs

Metal **springs** work in a way similar to elastic bands. If we pull on the ends of a spring we can stretch it. We can feel the spring pulling back on our hands. If we let go of the spring, it goes back to its original shape. If we push on the ends of the spring, we can feel it pushing back on our hands. If we let go of the spring, it goes back to its original shape.

The orange stretches the spring a little.

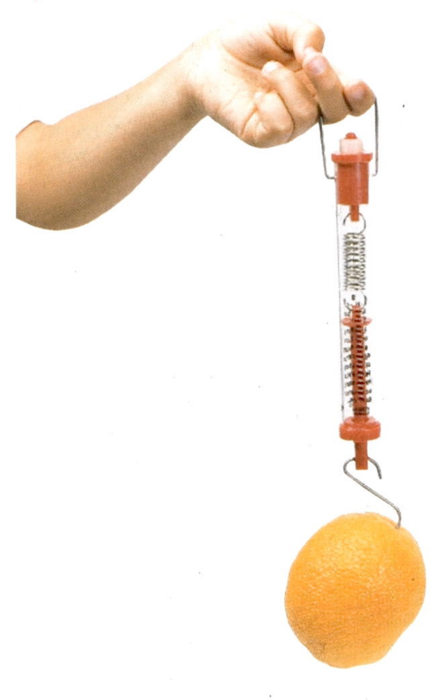

The bag of sugar stretches the spring much more.

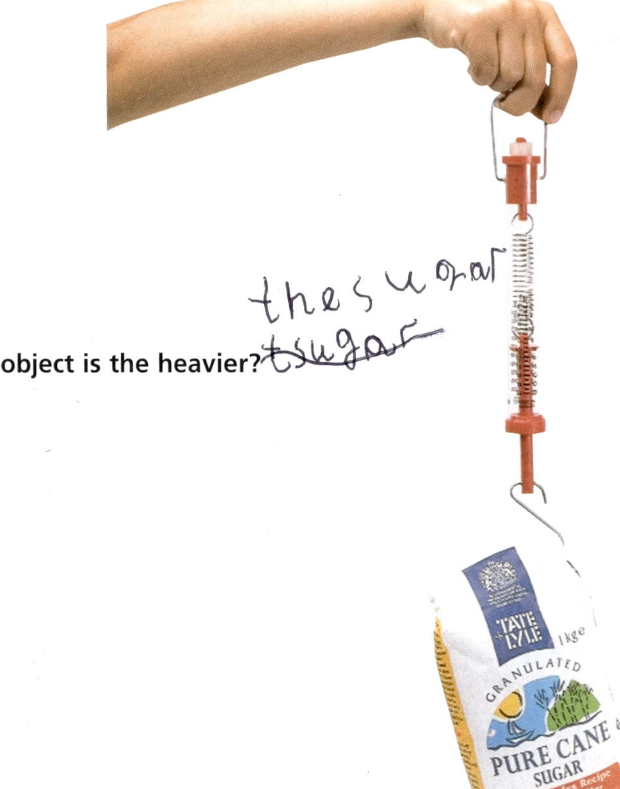

Which object is the heavier?

Using springs

Metal springs have many different uses. Staplers and some ballpoint pens have springs inside them. There are springs on motorcycles and cars to stop them being shaken by bumps in the road.

In a clockwork motor, a coiled-up strip of steel slowly unwinds to turn the wheels.

Leaf springs are used in some trucks. The 'leaves' are bendy strips of steel clamped together.

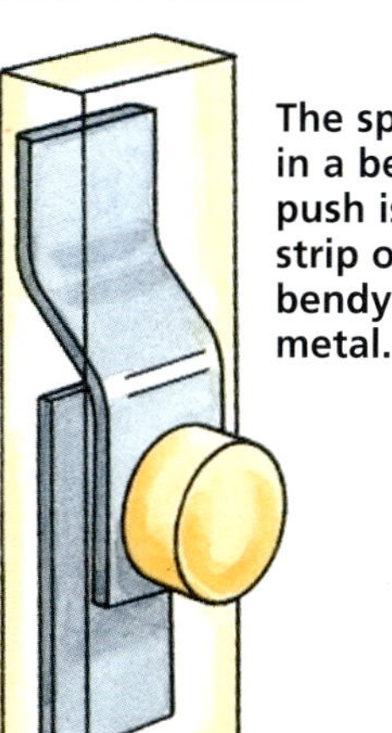

The spring in a bell-push is a strip of bendy metal.

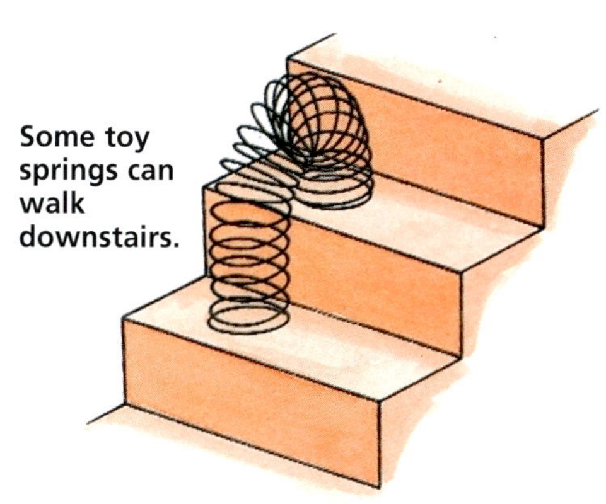

Some toy springs can walk downstairs.

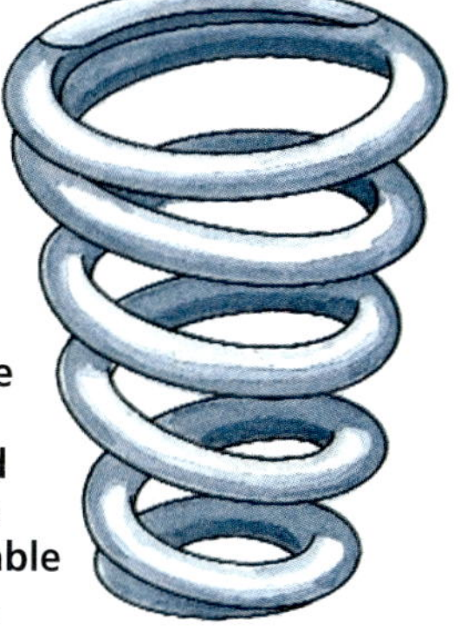

Coil springs are used in some mattresses and chairs to make them comfortable to lie or sit on.

These are a few of the ways in which we use springs.

Questions

1 a Make a collection of springs and draw them.

b Find a way to measure the force needed to stretch or squash each of them.

c Record your results. Is the biggest spring the hardest to pull or push?

2 Examine a weighing machine that works with springs. Draw it and label the parts. How does it work? Describe this in your own words.

3 How many everyday things can you think of that have a spring in them?

4 What happens when you pull on a spring? Draw a picture and use arrows to show the direction of the forces (pushes or pulls). Write down what is happening.

Light and shadows

If you stand with your back to the sun, you will see a dark patch on the ground in front of you. This is your **shadow**.

How many shadows can you see in this picture? How are they different from the bodies that are making them?

Shadows

Light from the sun travels only in straight lines, so it cannot bend and go around corners. A shadow forms when an object blocks some of the sun's light so that it cannot shine on the ground. Our shadow is roughly the same shape as our body because our body is blocking out the sunlight. When we move, our shadow moves with us.

How shadows are formed

When we shine a torch on to a large sheet of white paper in a darkened room, we see a circle of light on the paper. If we hold a pencil in the torchlight, we will see its shadow on the paper. The shadow is shaped like the pencil because no light can pass through it to shine on the paper.

You can make interesting shadows if you block out the light from a torch.

How many transparent objects can you see in this picture? How many opaque objects can you see? Which of these objects would form the darkest shadows?

Never look directly at the sun, even through sunglasses. It could damage your eyes.

Blocking out the light

All shadows are made because light is blocked by something. The darkest shadows are formed by opaque objects, like a pencil or your body, because no light can pass through them. But even transparent objects, like a glass bottle, block out a little light and form a shadow. The shadow will not be as dark as one formed by an opaque object because light can pass through transparent objects.

On a dull day, we do not see shadows because clouds scatter the sunlight in many directions.

Questions

1 How are shadows formed? Describe this in your own words. Draw a picture to help your explanation.

2 Do coloured lights form coloured shadows? Describe how you would find out for yourself.

3 Draw some shadows. Show them to your friends. Ask your friends to guess which objects made the shadows.

The sun and day and night

The sun is a **star**, just like the stars we see in the night sky. It is over a million times bigger than the Earth.

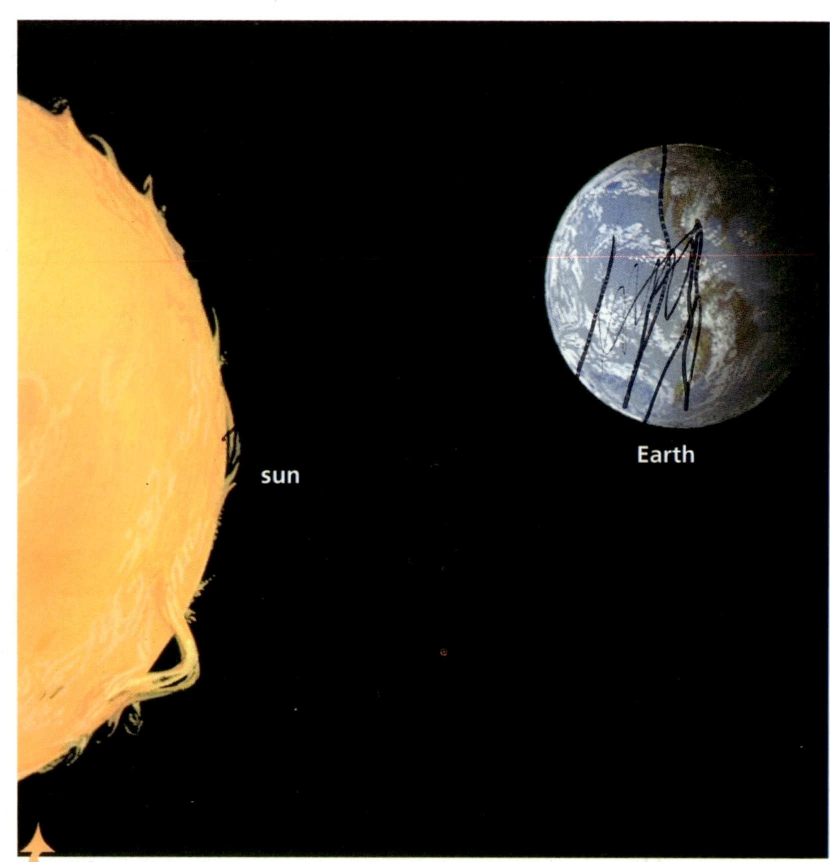

When it is day on one side of the Earth, it is night on the other side.

Heat and light from the sun

The sun is a huge ball of white-hot gases which give us light and heat. Without the sun, the Earth would be very cold and completely dark. Plants use the sunlight to make their food, and animals eat plants or animals that eat plants. So nothing would be able to live on the Earth without the sun's light and heat.

Never look directly at the sun, even through dark glasses. It could damage your eyes.

Night and day

During the day we see the light from the sun, but at night we cannot see the sun. This is because the Earth turns like a spinning top. It takes 24 hours for the Earth to turn once, and this turning causes night and day. It is day on the side of the Earth where the sun is shining. It is night on the other side which is in dark shadow. The sun seems to rise as our part of the Earth turns to face it at the beginning of the day. Night comes when our part of the Earth turns away from the sun.

A city street during the day.

The same street at night. What differences can you see?

Questions

1 Where is it night-time when it is daytime where you live? Use a globe to find out the names of the countries.

2 Look out of a window at the sky when it is dark. What you can see? Draw the sky.

3 Draw your house or school. Where is the sun in the morning? Draw it in your picture in yellow. Where is the sun at mid-day? Draw it in orange. Where is the sun in the evening? Draw it in red.

4 Draw a picture of the street where you live in the daytime. Draw another picture of your street at night. What things have changed in the second picture?

Telling the time with shadows

The Earth turns all the time and, because of this, the sun appears to us to move across the sky. The sun appears to be low down in the morning, overhead in the middle of the day and low again in the evening before it finally disappears.

Changing shadows

Because the sun tracks across the sky, the shadows it casts change. Shadows are longest first thing in the morning and in the late afternoon. They are shortest in the middle of the day. Not only do shadows get longer and shorter during the day, they also change direction.

On a sunny morning in the playground, ask a friend to draw around your feet and around your shadow with a piece of chalk. Stand in the same place in the middle of the day. Ask your friend to draw around your shadow now. Then do the same thing at the end of the afternoon. How have the length and direction of your shadow changed?

How has this girl's shadow moved during the day? Does the sun seem to be in the same place?

Sundials

Because shadows change direction we can use them to tell the time. A pointer or 'gnomon' on a **sundial** casts a shadow across the dial. The position of the shadow changes during the day as the sun appears to move across the sky.

Left: the sun is bright enough to cast a shadow between X and XI. What time might it be?
Right: the sun isn't bright enough to cast any shadow.

Questions

1 Look at a sunflower on a sunny morning. Look at it again later. See how the flower has turned to follow the sun!
  - **a** Look at daisies on a sunny day – in the morning and in the evening. How does the sun affect them?
  - **b** Which other flowers could you use to help you tell the time?

2 Mark where a patch of sunlight falls on the floor or wall of your classroom. Look for the patch an hour or two later. Has it moved? Why is this?

3 **a** Plan an investigation to make your own sundial. Try out your ideas on a sunny day.
  - **b** Can a shadow made by an artificial light, such as a torch or desk lamp, be used to tell the time? Discuss this with your friends.

Everyday rocks

We can see rocks on the slopes of a mountain.

The Earth is covered with **rocks**, but in many places the rocks are hidden by soil and plants. We can see rocks on the beach, on hillsides and in deserts. We can also see the rocks when we look at quarries or the cuttings made for roads and railways.

Building with rocks

Churches, gravestones and old buildings are often made of natural rocks shaped into blocks. Many statues and monuments are carved from rocks. Some paving-stones and kerbstones are made of natural rock that has been cut and shaped.

Artificial rocks

Natural rock can be changed or mixed with other things to make **artificial** rock. Concrete is an artificial rock. Bricks are made of baked clay which is powdered rock. Glass is made from melted sand which is tiny pieces of rock. Some roofs are covered with flat grey sheets of a rock called slate.

We can see the rocks in the cliffs by the sea.

More uses of rocks

People have used rocks to build their houses for thousands of years, but many other things also are made from rocks. Cement, tiles and pottery are made from rocks. Coal comes from rocks, and oil and gas are trapped in rocks. Talcum powder is made from talc which is found in rocks. Pumice stones are pieces of rock that came from volcanoes. Small pieces of a very hard rock called granite are used to surface roads. We also obtain metals and precious stones, such as diamonds, emeralds, rubies and sapphires, from rocks.

A stream uncovers rocks as it flows along.

Questions

1 Look around your school buildings. How many different rocks can you see? What are they being used for? Why are they being used in these places? Write a short account of what you have discovered.

2 Can you think of a way to test rocks to see if they absorb (soak up) water? How will you make your test fair? Try out your ideas to see if they work.

3 How do we use rocks? Make a book describing as many uses that you can find. Collect interesting pictures to illustrate your book.

Rocks under the surface

There are rocks underneath the surface everywhere on Earth, even under the oceans. In order to get the rocks that we use, we often have to dig large holes.

Stone for building is being cut from this quarry.

Sand, gravel and clay

Sand and clay are quite soft rocks. They are easily scooped out of the ground with mechanical diggers. Gravel is also dug from open pits. Some gravel pits are full of water so the gravel has to be sucked out through large pipes.

Sand and gravel pits, quarries and mines are dangerous. Keep away from them, unless you are on a special school visit.

Quarries

Larger lumps of rock come from special pits called **quarries**. In one kind of quarry, large blocks of rock are cut from the sides with special saws, drills and chisels. Granite, marble and slate are quarried like this. In some other quarries, explosives are used to produce broken-up pieces of rock, called **aggregate**. Aggregate is spread between railway lines and used to make roads.

Granite is a very hard rock. It is used for making buildings and surfacing roads.

We make iron and steel from iron ore.

The metal copper is made from malachite.

Many fine buildings are made from limestone.

Mining

Mining is the process of digging valuable materials out of the ground. When coal and iron **ore**, the rock from which iron and steel are made, are near the surface of the ground they are dug out by huge mechanical shovels. Some of the biggest machines in the world are used in this kind of mining.

Most gold and a lot of coal come from deep underground. These materials are mined by tunnelling. Drilling for oil and gas is also a form of mining. Oil and gas are usually found deep under the ground and in rocks under the sea.

Many statues are carved from marble.

Questions

1 Where can we find rocks? Collect pictures of scenery in which rocks can be seen. Include mountains, hills, river valleys, waterfalls, cliffs, beaches, caves, deserts, volcanoes and glaciers. Make a book or wall chart with your pictures.

2 How do rocks differ from place to place? Make a collection of rocks from everywhere you go. Wash and dry your rocks carefully. Label each one with the place and date on which you found it. Use books to try to find the names of your rocks.

3 Think about each of the objects or materials in the box. Which of them are made from rocks?

> glass jar knife salt pencil
> concrete post diamond ring
> brick lump of coal
> the plaster cast on a broken arm

What is soil?

Soil is found almost everywhere on land, although in rocky places and deserts there is often very little soil. Some soils may be too poor for most plants to grow in them. Other soils are good and grow many plants. These are called **fertile** soils.

The soil deep below the surface (the subsoil) is a lighter colour because it contains very little humus.

Soil from rocks

Soil is slowly being formed all the time. An important part of soil is made from rocks broken into tiny pieces by plant roots, water, ice, heat and cold, and the wind. Some types of soil are more fertile than others, depending on the rock they were made from. Water drains through some soils quicker than through others. Some plants grow better in one type of soil than in others.

Humus

When plants and animals die, they **decay** or rot and eventually form a black substance called **humus**. When a lot of humus is mixed in with tiny pieces, or grains, of rock, a soil has been formed.

Earthworms help to make the soil fertile.

Lichens grow on pieces of rock. When they die and decay they become mixed with tiny particles of rock. This forms soil in which other plants can grow.

A soil containing a lot of humus is fertile. The humus provides mineral salts for growing plants. Humus also helps the soil to hold water which plant roots can take up.

Questions

1 The soil on the tops of hills is often very shallow. On the lower slopes the soil is much deeper. What do you think is the reason for this?

2 Why do some farmers plough deeply into the soil?

3 Copy these statements. Think about them carefully. Put a tick (✔) next to the statements that are true. Put a cross (✘) next to the statements that are false.

a Soil is made of tiny pieces of rock.

b All plants need a thick layer of subsoil to grow in.

c Soil is a home for many animals.

d A fertile soil contains a lot of humus.

e Humus is formed from rotting pieces of rock.

Why is soil important?

Soil is valuable because all the plants we eat and get materials from grow in soil. The animals that provide us with food also eat plants that grow in the soil.

When leaves fall from the trees they decay and help to form humus.

Soil animals

Soil is a home for millions of animals. One gram of fertile soil may contain more than 1 million animals. Many of them are too small for us to see without a microscope, but there are also earthworms, ants, beetles, centipedes, millipedes and spiders. Larger animals, like foxes, badgers, rabbits and mice, make their burrows in the soil.

Ploughing and digging

Farmers plough the fields before they plant them. The plough turns the soil over to let in air so that the bacteria, plant roots and small animals can breathe and grow. **Weeds** are buried when the soil is ploughed, then they decay and mix with the soil to form humus.

All of our food crops, including oats from which some breakfast cereals and biscuits are made, are grown in soil.

In winter, water in the soil turns to ice and breaks lumps of soil into small pieces. Seeds grow better in the small pieces of soil. Gardeners use a spade to break the soil, to let air into it and to bury the weeds.

We plant seedlings in fertile soil to help them grow well.

Disappearing soil

Although we depend on soil for our food and many other things, every year much good soil is covered with buildings, concrete and roads. We must take care of the soil we have left because fertile soils take many thousands of years to form.

Questions

1 Mr Smith and Mrs Patel used seeds from the same packet to grow carrots in their gardens. Mrs Patel's carrots grew much better than Mr Smith's. Why did this happen? Give three reasons.

2 Plan an investigation to find out roughly how many earthworms there are in an area of soil. It would take too long to catch and count every single worm. What could you do instead?

3 If you wished to make a garden on the side of a hill, how would you stop the soil being washed away? Draw a picture showing what your garden would look like and how you would plant it.

Plants that feed us

Plants provide us with all our food, either directly or indirectly. The vegetables we eat are plants and the fruits we eat come from plants. Foods such as milk, meat and eggs come from animals that eat plants.

The fruits we eat come from plants. What are these fruits?

Useful grasses

Grasses grow everywhere. They provide food for many of the animals which give us meat and milk. Both wild and farm animals eat grass. In winter, many farm animals are fed on hay which is dried grass.

Cereals and their seeds. What do we use these cereals for?

Sugar cane is a kind of grass from which we get much of our sugar. Straw from cereals, and reeds which are also grasses, are used to make or thatch the roofs of some buildings.

Cereals

Wheat, oats and barley are all kinds of grasses. These food grasses are often called **cereals**. Rye, maize and rice are also cereals. The seeds of these important cereals provide food for people all over the world.

Wheat grains, the seeds of wheat, are ground into flour from which we make bread and cakes. Oat grains are ground to make oatmeal. Cornflakes are made from the grains of maize, and we eat rice boiled, baked or fried. Cereal grains are also important foods for chickens and some other farm animals.

Eating apples come from trees that have been developed from wild crab-apple trees.

Wild crab-apples.

Questions

1 Imagine that a disease is beginning to kill all kinds of grasses. What will happen? Discuss this with your friends.

2 Choose any country that you know about where cereal crops are grown. Draw or trace a map and mark on it the main cereal-growing areas. Why are most cereals grown in those areas?

3 Which cereal is used to make cornflakes? Find out where it is grown and how it is sown and harvested. Then do the same for rice.

4 Find out where and how flour is made. Draw pictures to show how flour is made. What is the difference between white flour and wholemeal flour?

The parts of a plant

Every living thing needs food to live. Plants can make their own food, but animals have to eat either plants or other, smaller animals which have eaten plants. All the food in the world comes directly or indirectly from plants.

Flowering plants usually have four main parts – roots, stems, leaves and flowers. Each part has a special job to do.

You can watch roots growing if you stand an onion on a jar of water.

Roots

The **roots** hold the plant firmly in the soil and stop the plant from blowing away in the wind. Roots also take in water and substances called **mineral salts**, which the plant needs to grow, from the soil.

Stems

The **stems** of a plant are like your skeleton because they help to support the parts of the plant that are above the ground. They hold the leaves and flowers up to the light. A stem also contains tiny tubes that carry food and water to different parts of the plant. The stem of a tree is called its **trunk**.

Leaves

Leaves are very important because they make the food for the whole plant. They have tiny holes, or **pores**, on their undersides. The air the plant needs and its waste gases pass through these pores. The pores also give off the water the plant does not need.

Leaves can be all shapes and sizes.

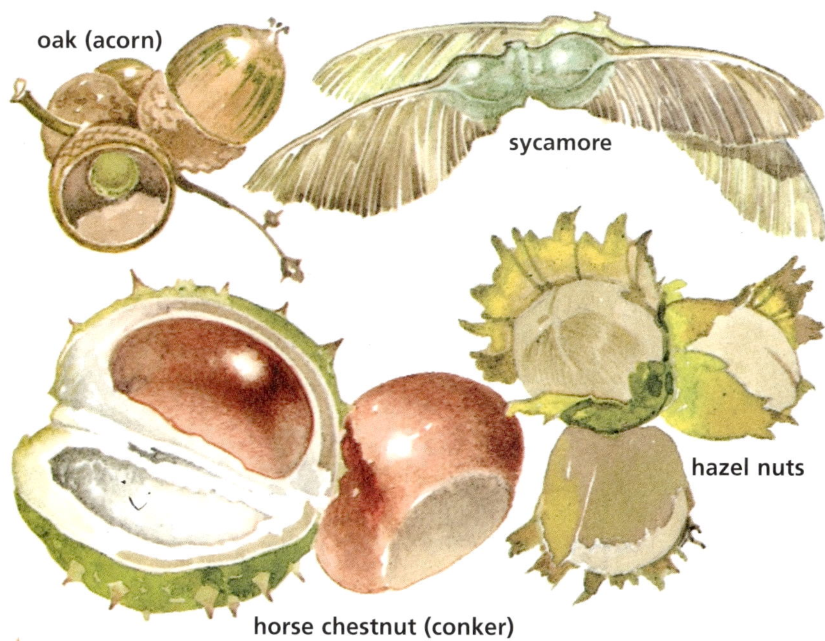

How do you think these seeds are scattered away from the trees on which they grew?

Plant leaves are green because they contain a special chemical that absorbs, or 'soaks up' sunlight. A plant kept in the dark will be pale and yellow because it will not make the green chemical.

Flowers

The **flowers** of a plant produce the fruits and seeds. The fruit protects the seeds and helps to scatter them. The seeds will eventually grow into new plants.

Questions

1 A weed is a plant that is growing where it is not wanted.
- **a** How many kinds of weeds can you think of? Make a list of them.
- **b** What kinds of plants are they? What do they all have in common?

2 Some plants store food. Write out a list of vegetables. For each vegetable say where it stores food. Is it in the roots, the stems, the leaves, or somewhere else? (For example, carrots store food in their roots.)

3 Draw a flowering plant. Label the parts of the plant with the letters described below.
- **a** Where the plant catches sunlight.
- **b** Where the plant takes up water.
- **c** Where the plant makes its fruits and seeds.
- **d** Where the plant makes its food.
- **e** Where the water and food travel to all parts of the plant.

4 How are fruits and seeds scattered away from the parent plant? Write about or draw pictures of all the ways you can find.

Why plants need water

Farmers water their crops in dry weather to make sure they grow well.

Like animals, plants need water in order to live. A plant uses water to make its food and to carry it to all parts of the plant.

Root hairs

Most plants get their water from rain that has soaked into the soil. The roots grow down into the soil and tiny roots, called **root hairs**, grow on the surface of the roots. They take up the water and dissolved mineral salts found in the soil.

Taproots and fibrous roots

There are two main types of root. A **taproot** is a single, thick root with smaller roots, covered in root hairs, growing on it. Some taproots, such as carrots, are swollen with stored food. Tiny tubes down the centre of the taproot carry water away from, and food to, the roots.

Plants, such as grasses, have masses of thin, spreading roots. These are called **fibrous roots**. Some trees have huge masses of fibrous roots which grow deep into the soil.

All plants need water if they are to grow, so we should give them water if there is no rain.

Few plants can grow in the desert because there is so little water. This plant stores water when it rains to use during the long periods of dry weather.

Using water

The water taken up by the roots passes along the stem of the plant in tiny tubes. It goes up to the leaves where some of it is used to make the plant's food. The rest **evaporates** from the leaves.

Water helps the plant's stems to be firm and upright and its leaves to stay flat. If a plant is not watered, it loses water from its leaves faster than water can be taken up from the soil. The stem and leaves of the plant become limp and we say the plant has **wilted**. If the plant does not get water, it will die.

Questions

1 Imagine you have bought a plant from the garden centre.
- **a** Draw a picture of the plant. Label the parts of the plant.
- **b** You forget to water your plant for a week. Does it look different? Draw it.
- **c** It is two months later and you have never watered the plant. Draw what your plant looks like now.

2 Fibrous roots spread out a long way. Taproots go deep underground and store food. Which of the following plants have fibrous roots and which have taproots?

runner bean   daisy   beetroot   radish   grass   carrot
apple tree   lettuce   parsnip   sunflower

3 What would happen to a plant if:
- **a** it was left on a sunny windowsill and not watered?
- **b** it was watered but left in the cold?
- **c** it was given water and kept warm, but left in the dark?
- **d** it was given the right amount of water, warmth and light?
- **e** it was given too much water?

Helping plants to grow

Plants need the right amount of sunshine and water to grow. They also need warmth and mineral salts from the soil. In countries with cold winters, farmers and gardeners usually sow seeds during the spring, when the weather is warmer. The plants grow during the summer. By the end of summer or early autumn, the plants are ready to harvest.

Sometimes farmers spread animal dung on the soil to help make it more fertile.

Making the soil fertile

When crops have been growing in the soil, there may not be many mineral salts left for new plants. Some farmers and gardeners spread straw or rotting plants, called **compost**, on the soil to make it more fertile.

Farmers plough their fields to break up the soil and bury the weeds.

Fertilizers

Some farmers and gardeners put chemical **fertilizers** on their soil. These chemical fertilizers produce mineral salts that the plants can use. But chemical fertilizers do not produce humus and so they do not help to improve the soil.

Plants grow well in the moist, warm and light conditions inside a greenhouse.

Greenhouses

Some farmers and gardeners grow food crops and flowering plants in greenhouses. This is because people need the same amount of food all the year round. Plants do not grow well in cold weather, but inside a greenhouse heaters keep the air warm. If the weather is not sunny there are special electric lights so that the plants can make their food. Water may be sprinkled on to the plants to keep the soil moist. Then the plants can grow quickly and healthily.

Questions

1. Pretend you have several plants, all of the same kind and size, growing in pots. How could you make your plants grow more quickly? Plan a fair investigation to answer the question.
2. Ben planted some radish seeds in his garden on a frosty day in winter. The seeds did not grow. Why do you think this was? Write a sentence or draw a diagram to explain your answer.
3. In what ways might animals help plants to grow? Discuss this with your friends.
4. Find out the names of some of the plants which grow on the ground in a wood. Why do you think that most of them grow and flower in the early spring rather than in the warmer days of summer?

Glossary

Activity Movement and exercise.

Aggregate Broken rock or gravel used in making concrete.

Artificial Not natural; made by people.

Attract To pull something with a power that cannot be seen.

Canine A pointed tooth, sometimes called a fang.

Cereal A grass plant that produces seeds used as food, such as wheat, maize or rice.

Compost Decaying plant leaves, stems and other materials used to fertilize and improve the soil.

Decay To go bad, to rot.

Diet Foods someone normally eats.

Electromagnet An iron bar, surrounded by a coil of wire, which becomes a magnet when electricity flows through the wire.

Energy The power and ability something has to do work.

Evaporate To change from a liquid to steam or vapour; to dry up.

Fat An energy-rich food. Butter, margarine and cooking oil are fats; milk, cheese and cream contain fats.

Fertile A good soil in which many plants can grow is said to be fertile.

Fertilizer A substance put on the soil to make plants grow better.

Fibre A tiny, fine thread; the part of fruits, vegetables and other plants we eat that cannot be digested.

Fibrous root One of a large mass of thin roots.

Flower The part of a plant which often has colourful petals. It is where the plant produces its fruits and seeds.

Force A push or pull.

Furnace A special fireplace for producing great heat.

Gum A sticky substance used as glue; the firm pink flesh around the teeth.

Humus Decayed animals and plants which are part of the soil.

Incisor A sharp, chisel-shaped front tooth used for biting and gnawing.

Leaf One of the flat, green growths where a plant makes its food.

Lens A transparent piece of glass or plastic through which things look either bigger or smaller.

Magnet A piece of metal which has the power to attract certain other kinds of metal, including iron and steel.

Magnetic Having the power of, or being attracted by, a magnet.

Manufactured material A material made by people.

Material Any substance from which something can be made.

Mining Digging or removing from underground materials such as coal or diamonds.

Mineral salt One of the chemical substances plants obtain from the soil and use as food; a substance in food that you need to stay healthy.

Molar One of the wide teeth at the back of your mouth.

Molten A material that has been melted.

Natural material A material that has not been made or changed by people.

Opaque Describes something that you cannot see through, and that does not let light through.

Ore A rock from which a metal can be extracted.

Plastic A light, manufactured material that can be made or moulded into different shapes.

Pole One end of a magnet.

Pore A tiny opening in a leaf or in the skin.

Power station A large building where electricity is produced.

Prey Animals that are hunted by other animals for food.

Property A characteristic of a material, such as 'hard', 'shiny'.

Quarry A large hole where rock is dug out of the ground.

Raw materials Materials which are used to make a new material.

Recycle To reuse a material.

Repel To drive or force something away.

Rock The solid part of the Earth's crust underneath the soil. Not all rocks are hard.

Root The part of a plant that normally grows under the ground.

Root hair One of the tiny hair-like roots which grow on a larger root.

Shadow A dark shape on a surface caused when something is placed in front of a light source.

Soil Tiny, loose particles of rock and humus.

Spring A bendy coil of metal.

Star One of the objects in space that you can see at night as small points of light. The sun is a star.

Starch An important part of your diet, which gives you energy.

Stem One of the main stalks of a plant.

Sundial A device that shows the time using a shadow made by the sun.

Taproot The main root of a plant that grows straight down.

Transparent Describes something you can see through.

Trunk The main stem of a tree.

Vitamin A substance in food that you need to stay healthy.

Weed A wild plant that is growing where it is not wanted.

Wilt When a plant loses its freshness and droops.

Index